THE KEYS TO CHRISTIAN LIVING

Understanding God's Spiritual Laws for Godliness

MICHAEL POWELL

Unless otherwise indicated, all Scripture quotations are taken from the openbible.info website, New King James Version (NKJV).

Time, Talent, Treasure, Testimony, and Touch are intellectual property of Opened Door Christian Fellowship in Laurie, Missouri, and Rev. Thom Jones. It has been approved for use in this publication.

The Keys to Christian Living/Understanding God's Spiritual Laws for Godliness

ISBN 13: 979-8-9871567-2-8 | eBook: 979-8-9871567-3-5

Living Vision Publishing books may be ordered at www.livingvisionpublishing.com.

For further information, please contact: www.livingvisionpublishing.com

Dedication

I dedicate this work to my lovey and precious bride, Juanita. You truly are a gift from God.

Acknowledgements

I am so thankful for the pastors, leaders, teachers, mentors, and friends that influenced my spiritual growth over the years. The lessons learned from their council along with the guidance of Holy Spirit has been invaluable to me. Thank you all for caring enough to give of yourself.

Table of Contents

Introduction

Over the many years I served in several different church ministries and thought I was carrying out God's calling on my life. I received great satisfaction in those years, but I didn't grow a whole lot spiritually, until recently the Lord instructed me to "finish well." Not just once, but He's telling me "finish well" over and over again. This makes sense.

I'm now in my senior years, and the Lord then gave me the idea to try a different ministry. "Lord, does this have anything to do with finishing well?" I asked. He said, "Yes it does!"

A few months later the Lord then placed in me the intense desire to mentor new believers right after they accept Jesus as their Savior. In Matthew 13:3-23 Jesus teaches on the "Parable of the Sower." This story keeps running through my mind like a broken record. The thought of a new believer not getting grounded in God's Word and backsliding back into the world now breaks my heart like never before.

After more prayer and conversations with my pastor, God gave me the idea to write a simple little book that teaches the new believer a few of the key godly principles found in the Bible the moment they finished the Sinner's Prayer. Wait a minute! Write a book? Are you crazy God?

No, God is not crazy. This little book will hopefully ground you, the new believer, with several Christian "best-practices" that will fortify your belief in God and provide you guidance to shoot Satan down when he attacks.

I pray this book quickly gives you the tools you need to start living a godly Christian life on a solid spiritual foundation. May you be richly blessed as you study the principles in this book.

Welcome to God's Family

I'd like to congratulate you for your decision to follow Christ! All heaven rejoices with your joining God's family. God designed a life for you, the Christian, that allows you to have a glorious relationship with Him and in return, your life will be blessed beyond comprehension. Bruce Wilkinson conveys this sentiment quite well in his book, "A Life God Rewards." Quoting Mr. Wilkinson, *"Our <u>belief determines where</u> we will spend eternity, and our <u>behavior determines how</u> we will spend eternity."* God wants to bless us here on earth and in heaven if we just give Him the BEST of ourselves.

The Bible is full of scriptures that describe God's life principles (spiritual laws) that can guide you to and through a blessed life. The non-believer says God has too many rules that keeps you from having fun and enjoying life. That's just not true! The Bible outlines God's strategy and plan for the Christian's well-being just as any loving earthly father would have for their children.

> ***"When anyone hears the word of the kingdom, and does not understand it, then the wicked one comes and snatches away what was sown in his heart..." (Matthew 13:19)***

Satan, a.k.a. "the evil one," is not happy you made the decision to follow Jesus. In fact, He's really ticked-off! Be on guard! Satan will make several attempts to "steal you back" into his lost world. This would be a great travesty!

It is my desire that you practice these godly principles, so they become an integral part of who you are. These principles will place you on solid spiritual ground that will help you ward off Satan's attacks and fill your life with tremendous joy and God's peace.

KEY #1:

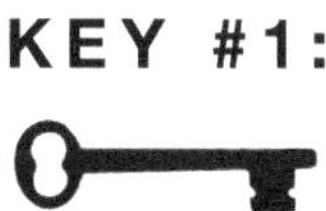

Do Everything with Love

"For God so loved the world, that he gave his only begotten Son…" (John 3:16)

"He who does not love does not know God, for God is love." (1 John 4:8)

What does it mean to love? Let's take a quick look at how the Greek language defines love.

Agape Love - Love without expecting anything in return (pleasing God)

Phileo Love - Brotherly love as you relate on the human level (pleasing others)

Eros Love - The love of self-gratification (pleasing yourself)

This is Key #1 for a very good reason. It must be the primary core belief and value that operates in a Christian's life. Every other key that follows in this book is dependent on the amount of agape love you have in your heart. It's that important! As a believer, you need to ask yourself one question daily, "Who am I trying to please? Myself, others, or God?

> *"For by grace you have been saved through faith, and that not of yourselves; it is the gift of God, not of works, least anyone should boast." (Ephesians 2:8-9)*

God's love for you is the ultimate expression of agape love. God gave His son to pay for your sins by dying on the cross and raising Him from the grave on the third day. You haven't earned His gift by your efforts (works) or good intentions. It's only by God's grace you are invited to receive His gift of salvation and eternal life and we rejoice that you did make that commitment.

> *"Blessed are the pure in heart, for they shall see God." (Matthew 5:8)*

The health of your spiritual heart is reflected in your desires, motivations, and actions every day. Your sinful nature will try to pull you back into a self-gratification (eros love) life. Your goal each day should be to live the day with agape love in your heart. God will bless you! As a new creature in Christ, you should want to please God in all that you say and do, not out of obligation to God, but out of your love for your Heavenly Father.

KEY #2:

Be a Disciple of Christ

"And they continued steadfastly in the apostles' doctrine and fellowship, in the breaking of bread, and in prayers." *(Acts 2:42)*

As a new believer, I'm sure you're eager to learn more about what it means to live a Christian life. You're now hungry to absorb anything you can read or hear just to get started. Well, that's good! But what about a year from now? Three years from now?

"All Scripture is given by inspiration of God, and is profitable for doctrine, for reproof, for correction, for instruction in righteousness…" *(2 Timothy 3:16)*

Try to keep the desire to become more like Jesus alive in your heart every day! It's that simple! The moment you lose the desire to learn, your spiritual growth begins to decay. You may go through good seasons and poor so don't get discouraged if you find yourself in a learning slump. Just commit yourself to learn about Christ for the rest of your life. When you do, God will bless you with His peace and understanding, and in turn, He will equip you for ministry in His church.

"Then Jesus said to those Jews who be-lieved Him, "If you abide in My word, you are My disciples indeed. And you shall know the truth, and the truth shall make you free." (John 8:31-32)

As a disciple, you need to stay close to Jesus! He is the source of life. In John 15:1-11, Jesus instructs his disciples to "abide in Me." Simply put, we are the branches, He is the vine. How do the branches produce fruit? By staying attached to the vine and drawing nutrients and strength to produce good fruit. Likewise, we too need to abide in Jesus to gain our spiritual strength, so we produce good fruit here on earth.

"If you love me, keep my commandments."
(John 14:15)

Knowing what God wants you to do is not enough. Living to obey God gives you tremendous joy and free-dom. The world tells you obeying God is to obey an impossible set of rules. This is a lie from Satan! Your Father in heaven always has your best interest in mind. God wants you to benefit from His wisdom if you only listen and act as He speaks to you.

"Therefore whoever hears these sayings of Mine, and does them, I will liken him to a wise man who built his house on the rock: and the rain descended, the floods came, and the winds blew and beat on that house; and it did not fall, for it was founded on the rock. But everyone who hears these sayings of Mine, and does not do them, will be like a foolish man who built his house on the sand: and the rain descended, the floods came, and the winds blew and beat on that house; and it fell. And great was its fall." (Matthew 7:24-27)

"Not forsaking the assembling of ourselves together, as is the manner of some, but exhorting one another, and so much the more as you see the Day approaching." (Hebrews 10:25)

As a disciple you need to make church attendance a priority in your life. You'll be glad you did. The church body is your spiritual family and is a safe place to attend a Bible study for a deeper discussion of the scriptures. A Bible study also allows you the opportunity to ask questions.

"All Scripture is given by inspiration of God, and is profitable for doctrine, for reproof, for correction, for instruction in righteousness. . ." (2 Timothy 3:16)

As a disciple of Jesus, you need to read your Bible. The Bible is God's love letter to the believer. Every word in the Bible is God inspired and true! To doubt this gives Satan the opportunity to steal and possibly destroy your life! The more you read your Bible, the more you learn about God's character and His plan for your life. The promises of God still apply today! Trust that God will speak to you directly from His scriptures.

The Bible is divided into two major sections; the Old Testament (Genesis though Malachi) is the original covenant or agreement from God with the Israelites before Jesus' birth and the New Testament (Matthew through Revelation) is the current covenant God has for us to live by. The New Testament is also divided into two sections: The Gospels (Matthew, Mark, Luke, and John) and Christian Life Letters (Acts through Revelation).

> *"This Book of the Law shall not depart from your mouth, but you shall meditate in it day and night, that you may observe to do according to all that is written in it. For then you will make your way prosperous, and then you will have good success."*
> *(Joshua 1:8)*

Start your Bible journey by reading the book of John. When you finish John, ask God where He wants you to read next. Keep the majority of your reading in the New Testament, Proverbs, and the Psalms. Reading goals or plans rarely work in your favor and can become "legalistic" if you miss a few days. Instead, keep your reading time simple. Read the scriptures until God speaks to you specifically from a verse. Meditate on that verse or set of verses and ask God how you need to apply the spiritual truth in your life. Write notes in your Bible next to the scriptures that speak to you. Keep a notebook with your Bible so you can make notes when God speaks to you on Sunday mornings and the bible classes you attend.

KEY #3:

Pray Always

"Be anxious for nothing, but in every-thing by prayer and supplication, with thanksgiving, let your requests be made known to God; and the peace of God, which surpasses all understanding, will guard your hearts and minds through Christ Jesus." (Philippians 4:6-7)

Keep it simple when you pray. Have a conversation with your Heavenly Father. Talk to Him just like you talk with your best friend. No appointment needed! God is ALWAYS available to listen and talk and be sure to take time to be quiet and listen to God in your spirit. When you bring your cares and concerns to Him in prayer you no longer need to carry the load of worry. As you pray, God's peace will flood your spirit. You think God likes to bless you when to talk with Him? Of course He does! Your relationship with God will flourish the more you talk with your Heavenly Father. Jesus gave us a great prayer example.

> *"Pray then like this: 'Our Father in heaven, hallowed be Your name. Your kingdom come, Your will be done, on earth as it is in heaven. Give us this day our daily bread, and forgive us our debts, as we forgive our debtors. And do not lead us into temptation but deliver us from the evil one.'"*
> *(Matthew 6:9-13)*

There are three interesting elements in Jesus' prayer.

1. **Acknowledge God's presence**
   "Father in heaven" (Matthew 6:9)

2. **Adore Him** "Hallowed be Your name"
   (Matthew 6:9)

3. **Ask Him** "Your kingdom come; your
   will be done" (Matthew 6:10-13)

This is not a formula, but it does reflect Jesus' heart as He spoke to His Father. When you pray, keep it simple and pray as the Holy Spirit prompts you. Keep a journal of your prayer requests and the answered prayers. Occasionally go back and read your journal and reflect on how God answers your prayers. You will be amazed!

KEY #4:

Share Your Story

"...Go into all the world and preach the gospel to every creature." (Mark 16:15)

Witness! Share with others YOUR story of God's grace in your life. How has God changed you? How has God blessed you? How has God carried you through tough times? Sharing your story, even if you just tell someone that God loves them just as they are, plants spiritual seeds with non-believers that could get someone to start thinking about receiving Jesus in their life.

Develop your approach to start a conversation with strangers. Be yourself! Let the Holy Spirit guide your conversation. He will prompt you when to introduce the other person "your Jesus." Remember, as you share your story and your faith, your mission is to show others Jesus is alive in your life and He can make a positive difference for them too!

Be observant! Look for opportunities to help someone our just brighten there day with a smile or a cheerful greeting. Listen to the Holy Spirit! He will tell you what you need to do. Be sure log your experience so you can read later how God helped you help others.

KEY #5:

Fellowship with Other Believers

"Not forsaking the assembling of ourselves together, as is the manner of some, but exhorting one another..." (Hebrews 10:25)

If you remember, I talked about fellowshipping with the believers in Key #2 - Be a Disciple of Christ. I believe fellowship with other believers is important enough for a deeper discussion.

Fellowshipping with other believers is crucial for your spiritual growth but also crucial for your service back to the body. Make church attendance a priority in your week. You need the contact with fellow believers to encourage you and likewise encourage them. Attend a Bible class or a home group where you can develop personal relationships with others. These relationships will carry you through the good and bad times. As you develop close personal relationships, you'll be able to share specific prayer requests and encourage each other.

If you are married, commit to meeting during the day for time of devotional scripture reading and prayer. My wife and I have been doing a daily devotion together for several years now. The devotion and prayer take about ten to fifteen minutes of our time and we both are richly blessed when we start our day with Him. If you're single, I'd like to encourage you to start doing a daily devotional along with your regular scripture readings. There is a great variety of Christian devotionals available in written form or even downloadable as an application on your phone.

Fellowshipping with your church congregation allows you to give your five "Ts" (Time, Talent, Treasure, Testimony, and Touch). Let's take a closer look at the Five Ts.

TIME - God has given us all a limited supply of days in our life to work, go to school, fellowship, sleep, and eat. The things we can do with our time is endless! As believers, we all have the opportunity to serve God, our church, and our neighbors by investing our minutes, hours, and days doing God's work. Giving your time blesses not only God but you and those around you.

TALENT - God has gifts you with at least one talent, maybe more! He gave us this talent to bless the church body and the lost. Your talent is not just limited to bible teaching or singing in the choir! Your talent may be a skill like carpentry or painting. It might be administrative like bookkeeping. You might be able to lead and organize people during a community project. Whatever talent(s) you possess, don't squander, or hoard them! Share them so others can be blessed too.

TREASURE - Treasure is normally associated with your money. But your treasure is really anything you possess is considered treasure. Giving people cash, buying the groceries, filling up their car with gas is giving your treasure. You may give someone a new piece of furniture. That's treasure too! Treasure is something tangible you can give to someone or the church.

TESTIMONY - Your testimony is sharing your experience or history with God (see Key #4). How has God sustained you during tough time? How has God recently blessed you? Your witness is a gift to the non-believer and the believer both! Be sure to share the goodness of God with others as opportunities arise.

TOUCH - Touch is so much more than physically touching another person. Touch is relational. How do you relate with other people around you? Think of touch (relationship) as "being with" the other person as you talk. When you have a conversation, listen carefully and with purpose. Don't talk until the other person is done with their thought. Touch can also be a physical touch. Some people don't like to be touched and others thrive on it. Just be sensitive to the possibility a person may not want to be touched in that moment.

KEY #6:

Forgive Yourself and Others

"But if you do not forgive men their trespasses, neither will your Father forgive your trespasses." (Matthew 6:15)

"Bearing with one another, and forgiving one another, if anyone has a complaint against another; even as Christ forgave you, so you also must do." (Colossians 3:13)

Not forgiving others gives Satan the opportunity to kill your spiritual growth. Don't let resentment, grow into resistance, which grows into revenge or even hate. Deal with unforgiveness early before you or others are hurt. Remember, God has forgiven your sins against Him, you need forgive yourself first and others as Holy Spirit reveals unforgiveness in your heart. Your entire faith is based on practicing forgiveness. Be thankful for the forgiveness of sins you did not deserve and the restitution you could not pay.

Forgiveness is not optional. Jesus clearly addresses this in Matthew 18:22-35.

"Jesus said to him, "I do not say to you, up to seven times, but up to seventy times seven. Therefore the kingdom of heaven is like a certain king who wanted to settle accounts with his servants. And when he had begun to settle accounts, one was brought to him who owed him ten thousand talents. But as he was not able to pay, his master commanded that he be sold, with his wife and children and all that he had, and that payment be made. The servant therefore fell down before him, saying, 'Master, have patience with me, and I will pay you all.' Then the master of that servant was moved with compassion, released him, and forgave him the debt. But that servant went out and found one of his fellow servants who owed him a hundred denarii; and he laid hands on him and took him by the throat, saying, 'Pay me what you owe!' So his fellow servant fell down at his feet and begged him, saying, 'Have patience with me, and I will pay you all.' And he would not, but went and threw him into prison till he should pay the debt. So when his fellow servants saw what had been done, they were very grieved, and came and told their master all that had been done. Then his master, after he had called him, said to him, 'You wicked servant! I forgave you all that debt because you begged me. Should you not also have had compassion on your fellow servant, just as I had pity on you?' And his master was angry, and delivered him to the torturers until he should pay all that was due to him. So My heavenly Father also will do to you if each of you, from his heart, does not forgive his brother his trespasses." (Matthew 18:22:35)

KEY #7:

Honor God with Your Tithes and Offerings

"Honor the Lord with your possessions, and with the first fruits of all your increase; so your barns will be filled with plenty, And your vats will overflow with new wine." (Proverbs 3:9-10)

God **does not** need your money; He wants your heart! Here's a spiritual truth, God wants you to trust Him in all things, even your finances. When you tithe, you're giving back to Him your first fruits from your income. In return, God then blesses, He even multiplies the remaining 90 percent! You'll be amazed how blessed your life will be when you honor God with your tithes and offerings.

"Will a man rob God? Yet you have robbed Me! But you say, 'In what way have we robbed You?' In tithes and offerings. You are cursed with a curse, For you have robbed Me, Even this whole nation. Bring all the tithes into the storehouse, That there may be food in My house, And try Me now in this," Says the Lord of hosts,

> ***"If I will not open for you the windows of heaven And pour out for you such blessing That there will not be room enough to receive it." (Malachi 3:8-10)***

Just the opposite happens when you hold back your tithes. You're subconsciously telling God that you don't trust Him to provide for your needs. Be careful! There is a negative effect if you don't tithe! So many believers say, "I can't afford to give a tithe." When you don't give back to God what belongs to Him (your first fruits), the money you do keep, or hold back, doesn't go as far to cover your expenses which causes you even more stress and worry. Go ahead and test God! You have His permission! Take that step of faith and trust God will provide for your needs by committing to giving your tithe when you get paid. In return, God blesses the remaining ninety percent as He has promised. There's also an added bonus! You'll be blessed with unspeakable joy knowing you are in God's will.

> ***"For the earth is the Lord's, and all its fullness." (1 Corinthians 10:26)***

Everything you possess belongs to God. Once you understand who's the owner, you can then accept the fact you are His steward with the job to wisely manage His property and assets.

> ***"For to everyone who has, more will be given, and he will have abundance; but from him who does not have, even what he has will be taken away." (Matthew 25:29)***

God wants you to skillfully manage the assets and your talents you have been entrusted. Again, you are called to be an excellent steward over what you have been given. If you manage your affairs well, God will bless even more! Waste what you've been given, and you can surely expect a decrease.

> *"Give, and it will be given to you; good measure, pressed down, shaken together, and running over will be put into your bo- som. <u>For with the same measure that you use, it will be measured back to you...</u>" (Luke 6:38)*

This scripture is often associated with the giving of your treasure, also known as money. This key applies to all that you manage. To be a gracious giver you need to make sure your motivation to give is from agape love and not from eros or selfish reasons (see Key #1). Agape giving allows you to feely free give and not regret it later.

Be aware there's a negative effect that can be derived from this scripture too. If you argue, yell, or even hate oth- ers, these things will be returned to you in the same mea- sure. If you're receiving negative treatment, check your heart. This may be an indicator your heart is in eros mode. Pray and ask the Lord for His forgiveness and choose to move on with an agape love.

> *"So let each one give as he purposes in his heart, not grudgingly or of necessity; for*

God loves a cheerful giver." (2 Corinthians 9:7)

God wants to bless us with the riches of heaven so we can bless others. When you do give, thank God for His provision and the opportunity to bless others. Don't let regret entering your mind after you give. Any regret will steal your joy. Just focus on the graciousness of God that allowed you to be a blessing to someone.

Stretch your trust in God's provision by supporting missionaries or local Christian organizations. Holy Spirit will guide and speak to your heart when He wants you to participate outside your regular church giving.

"But he who is greatest among you shall be your servant." (Matthew 23:11)

Your time and talent can also be given back to your local church and charities. Ask God to show you where He wants you to serve. You will be amazed how much joy and satisfaction you receive as you are obedient when you serve in God's kingdom.

KEY #8:

There's a Spiritual War

"For we do not wrestle against flesh and blood, but against principalities, against powers, against the rulers of the darkness of this age, against spiritual hosts of wickedness in the heavenly places." (Ephesians 6:12)

We are in a spiritual battle! Satan has not given up on taking you back into his evil world. This spiritual battle is going on right now in heaven. Never forget this!

We all at times get lax in keeping our guard up against evil. Stay away from astrology, fortune telling, Ouija boards, or Tara cards. These things are the first step towards very evil practices such as witchcraft and Satanic worship. BEWARE! Run away from these satanic temptations. Stay on guard! Satan is continually trying to penetrate your spiritual defenses to gain a toehold in your life again. Build up your defense by reading your Bible, praying, and fellowshipping with other believers. You can always seek guidance and confess the temptation with your pastors and church leaders.

JESUS HAS ALREAD WON THE SPIRITUAL WAR WITH SATAN BY HIS DEATH ON THE CROSS AND HIS RESURRECTION!

We win! It's that simple! Know this and lean on this truth when you're under attack! If you do slip into sin, God is ALWAYS waiting for you to come back to His open arms if you only ask Him for forgiveness! "Stay on guard" needs to be your battle cry.

> ***"...do not be conformed to this world, but be transformed by the renewing of your mind, that you may prove what is that good and acceptable and perfect will of God." (Romans 12:2)***

You are new creature in Christ when you accept Jesus. Hopefully, you now have the deep desire to be transformed and fill your life with Godly and pure things. Likewise, filling your mind with negative thoughts and images can be a detriment on your spiritual health and happiness.

Keeping one foot in "the world" may be hindering you right now. This is where the Holy Spirit and your discernment (your understanding) come in. Some people need to make a clean break from the worldly life, so they don't fall completely back into the old lifestyle again. Some people think they can mix the Christian "good things" with some of their favorite secular music or movies and be just fine. That may be true for them. YOU need to decide for yourself what behaviors are best for your long-term spiritual growth.

Maybe it's time to be honest with yourself. Evaluate how things you "take in" effect you, good or bad. Ask yourself, what movies am I watching? What pictures am I looking at? What music or talk am I listening to? What is acceptable to God? How much of the world I'm living in is not acceptable to God? Can I balance some of the world and a Christian life? Know this. The health of your Christian life is just like eating a good healthy diet. If you add more of the good things from God into your life and minimize the things of the world you used to do, the better off you'll be in the long run.

In Romans 2:12 we are to be "transformed" in our minds. Pray and ask God to reveal and give you the discernment to know what things you need to eliminate or add to your life. Then you need take the necessary steps to make those changes a permanent part of your life.

> *"Whoever abides in Him does not sin. Whoever sins has neither seen Him nor known Him." (I John 3:6)*

If you expect to live your life as "the perfect Christian," you will surely be disappointed. Jesus was the only one who could live a sinless life! As a Christian, you will struggle with your flesh wanting to sin even if you desire to do what is right.

> *"If we confess our sins, he is faithful and just to forgive us our sins and to cleanse us from all unrighteousness." (1 John 1:9)*

Praise God our sins are already forgiven! This does not give us permission to willfully sin, but if we do, we need to confess the sin to God, and He will forgive us. Practice righteousness everyday by making it a priority to be more like Jesus in everything you say and do.

KEY #9:

Stay Vigilant

"Be sober, be vigilant; because your adversary the devil walks about like a roaring lion, seeking whom he may devour." (1 Peter 5:8)

This key goes hand-in-hand with the previous key, "There's a Spiritual War!" As a disciple you need to stay vigilant and ready for spiritual warfare. The scripture above (1 Peter 5:8) describes Satan as a lion that skillfully separates the weak from the herd to be eaten. By staying vigilant, you will be ready for the spiritual attacks when they come your way. The Bible speaks about three main reasons why we need to stay vigilant.

1. We don't know when Christ will return for His bride, the church.

2. We need to jump into action as Holy Spirit speaks to us to serve or give.

3. We need to weed-out and ignore false teachings.

Point number three is very important. You need to be able to discern what is truth and what is a lie. First and foremost, learn all about God's character and nature. Get to KNOW God as you would your best friend. Your ability to discern a lie from truth will become second nature to you the more you get to know God, your Father. Research the scriptures for life's answers. You'll be amazed how God provides the exact answer in His scriptures. Before you know it, you'll be able to quickly evaluate in your spirit what is truth and what is a lie.

Scrutinize what you hear, whether it's in church, on the television, or even social media by referring to the scriptures for the truth when something doesn't sound right in your spirit. The Holy Spirit will give you discernment to recognize when a teaching may not be in the Bible. If you still can't discern the truth, then seek a meeting with your pastor and ask for clarification. Present your question to your pastor "with love and compassion." If the discrepancy still can't be explained well enough to your satisfaction, ask the Lord to give you a deeper understanding of the truth and His wisdom.

KEY #10:

Walk with Integrity

"To do righteousness and justice is more acceptable to the Lord than sacrifice." *(Proverbs 21:3)*

A disciple needs to be a person with high integrity and a clean reputation. Your actions and words build your reputation as a person who can be trusted. Simple things like doing what you say you're going do when you say you're going to do it builds your reputation with others as a person they can trust and depend upon. Likewise, not doing what you say you're going to do has the opposite effect.

"But let your 'Yes' be 'Yes,' and your 'No,' 'No.' For whatever is more than these is from the evil one." (Matthew 5:37)

Of course, you want to speak truth and not mislead or deceive others. This goes without saying. Your actions, also known as your witness, speaks volumes about your Christian walk and character to people around you.

"And whatever you do, do it heartily, as to the Lord and not to men," (Colossians 3:23)

Let your life reflect the truth and love of Jesus in all you do whether it's your job, your schoolwork, or house chores. God gave His best at the cross. You need to give your best effort too!

KEY #11:

Life and Church Balance

"...do you not know that your body is a temple of the Holy Spirit within you, whom you have from God? You are not your own, for you were bought with a price. So, glorify God in your body." (1 Corinthians 6:19-20)

We have all been blessed with a wonderfully "God-designed" body. You need to take care your body and give it the food and rest to stay healthy. There may be times when you sense you're tired, either mentally, physically, or both. God rested on the seventh day (Genesis 2:1-3) and you need to be just as diligent to schedule rest time too.

Your church ministries and activities need to stay in balance with the other aspects in your life. Being over-committed with church activities and responsibilities is just as much a problem as not serving the church at all. Ask God to direct you on how to strike a balance in all aspects of your life (church, family, work or school, and recreation/relaxation).

Be aware there may be times when you may need to graciously respond with a "no thank-you, not at this time" when asked to add another ministry to your full schedule. Pray and ask God to give you guidance anytime you're considering adding any commitment to your schedule. Also consider the possibility God may be asking you to leave a ministry to move on to another or just take some time off to rest for a season. In either case, God will always guide your path if you only ask.

KEY #12:

God of Opposites

"And whoever exalts himself will be humbled, and he who humbles himself will be exalted." (Matthew 23:12)

Our behavior often is completely opposite from what God has intended for us. We act is selfish and self-serving ways that don't honor Him and in the long run, lead us down the path of destruction or at least, stagnation in our spiritual growth. That's not being blessed! Unfortunately, we too often follow our first thought or have a "fleshly reaction" when solving our own problems instead of considering and acting upon God's instructions.

Robert Morris covers this principle so well in his book, "The Blessed Life." *"God is a God of order. God doesn't think His order is the "right way" or the "best way"—* He thinks it's the **only way!** *He has an order for how we are to approach certain things and He wants His order to be accomplished."* Pastor Morris continues, **"...you must understand that God operates in opposites.** *His plan is always the opposite of our plan. If someone, does you wrong,* *you plan to tell him off. You go through the conversation in your mind, planning exactly what you're going to say to him. According to God, all that planning is time and energy wasted, because His plan—the opposite of yours—is to forgive your offender, act as if it never happened, and bless him. God's law of opposites says that **if you want to have authority, you must be under authority. If you want to receive, you must give. If you want to be first, you must be last. If you want to live, you must die to self.***"

> ***"...Assuredly, I say to you, unless you are converted and become as little children, you will by no means enter the kingdom of heaven." (Matthew 18:3)***

Again, Jesus is directing us in the opposite direction we would naturally head. We want to be the adult, in control, in command of the situation. But Jesus smacks that thinking down swiftly in Matthew 18:3. Jesus tells us to "become like children." What? And lose my position of being in control? No way! God wants us to be humble, have a child-like curiosity, and be completely dependent on Him as our Heavenly Father just like little children would with their earthly father.

Conclusion

We have only scratched the surface discussing the keys contained in the Bible. God has hundreds of principles for Christian living scattered throughout His scriptures. It is truly amazing. You can read a scripture, then read the same scripture again weeks later and God will speak something completely different to you. I sincerely hope and pray you practice the keys presented and add new keys as God reveals them to you.

> *"Looking unto Jesus, the author and finisher of our faith, who for the joy that was set before Him endured the cross, despising the shame, and has sat down at the right hand of the throne of God." (Hebrews 12:2)*

Keeping your eyes on Jesus helps you stay on the righteous path. God doesn't promise you won't go through hard times or trials. Remember this! When times do get tough you have the Holy Spirit living inside you to comfort you. Give the trial back to God in prayer. Ask for His help and God will move on your behalf.

May God richly bless your spiritual walk with Him. Enjoy the journey!

www.ingramcontent.com/pod-product-compliance
Lightning Source LLC
Chambersburg PA
CBHW041652150726
48005CB00013BA/1700